Sip...

Winery name

Winery location

Wine I tasted	*I liked it, or not*	*Price per bottle*
	☺ 😐 ☹	$
	☺ 😐 ☹	
	☺ 😐 ☹	
	☺ 😐 ☹	
	☺ 😐 ☹	
	☺ 😐 ☹	
	☺ 😐 ☹	
	☺ 😐 ☹	
	☺ 😐 ☹	
	☺ 😐 ☹	

People I met

Notes

Sip . Smile . Write . Repeat

Sip . Smile . Write . Repeat

Winery name

Winery location

Wine I tasted	I liked it, or not	Price per bottle
	☺ 😐 ☹	$
	☺ 😐 ☹	
	☺ 😐 ☹	
	☺ 😐 ☹	
	☺ 😐 ☹	
	☺ 😐 ☹	
	☺ 😐 ☹	
	☺ 😐 ☹	
	☺ 😐 ☹	
	☺ 😐 ☹	

People I met

Notes

Sip . Smile . Write . Repeat

Sip . Smile . Write . Repeat

Winery name
___

Winery location
___

Wine I tasted	I liked it, or not	Price per bottle
	😊 😐 ☹	$
	😊 😐 ☹	
	😊 😐 ☹	
	😊 😐 ☹	
	😊 😐 ☹	
	😊 😐 ☹	
	😊 😐 ☹	
	😊 😐 ☹	
	😊 😐 ☹	
	😊 😐 ☹	

People I met
___

Notes
___
___

Sip . Smile . Write . Repeat

Sip . Smile . Write . Repeat

Winery name

___

Winery location

___

Wine I tasted	I liked it, or not	Price per bottle
	😊 😐 ☹	$
	😊 😐 ☹	
	😊 😐 ☹	
	😊 😐 ☹	
	😊 😐 ☹	
	😊 😐 ☹	
	😊 😐 ☹	
	😊 😐 ☹	
	😊 😐 ☹	
	😊 😐 ☹	

People I met

___

Notes

___

Sip . Smile . Write . Repeat

Sip . Smile . Write . Repeat

Winery name

Winery location

Wine I tasted	I liked it, or not	Price per bottle
	😊 😐 ☹	$
	😊 😐 ☹	
	😊 😐 ☹	
	😊 😐 ☹	
	😊 😐 ☹	
	😊 😐 ☹	
	😊 😐 ☹	
	😊 😐 ☹	
	😊 😐 ☹	
	😊 😐 ☹	

People I met

Notes

Sip. Smile. Write. Repeat

Sip . Smile . Write . Repeat

Winery name

Winery location

Wine I tasted	I liked it, or not	Price per bottle
	☺ 😐 ☹	$
	☺ 😐 ☹	
	☺ 😐 ☹	
	☺ 😐 ☹	
	☺ 😐 ☹	
	☺ 😐 ☹	
	☺ 😐 ☹	
	☺ 😐 ☹	
	☺ 😐 ☹	
	☺ 😐 ☹	

People I met

Notes

Sip . Smile . Write . Repeat

Sip . Smile . Write . Repeat

Winery name
_____

Winery location
_____

Wine I tasted	I liked it, or not	Price per bottle
	😊 😐 ☹	$
	😊 😐 ☹	
	😊 😐 ☹	
	😊 😐 ☹	
	😊 😐 ☹	
	😊 😐 ☹	
	😊 😐 ☹	
	😊 😐 ☹	
	😊 😐 ☹	
	😊 😐 ☹	

People I met
_____

Notes
_____
_____

Sip . Smile . Write . Repeat

Sip . Smile . Write . Repeat

Winery name

Winery location

Wine I tasted	I liked it, or not	Price per bottle
	☺ 😐 ☹	$
	☺ 😐 ☹	
	☺ 😐 ☹	
	☺ 😐 ☹	
	☺ 😐 ☹	
	☺ 😐 ☹	
	☺ 😐 ☹	
	☺ 😐 ☹	
	☺ 😐 ☹	
	☺ 😐 ☹	

People I met

Notes

Sip. Smile. Write. Repeat

Sip . Smile . Write . Repeat

Winery name

_____

Winery location

_____

Wine I tasted	I liked it, or not	Price per bottle
	☺ 😐 ☹	$
	☺ 😐 ☹	
	☺ 😐 ☹	
	☺ 😐 ☹	
	☺ 😐 ☹	
	☺ 😐 ☹	
	☺ 😐 ☹	
	☺ 😐 ☹	
	☺ 😐 ☹	
	☺ 😐 ☹	

People I met

_____

Notes

_____

_____

Sip . Smile . Write . Repeat

Sip . Smile . Write . Repeat

Winery name

Winery location

Wine I tasted	I liked it, or not	Price per bottle
	☺ 😐 ☹	$
	☺ 😐 ☹	
	☺ 😐 ☹	
	☺ 😐 ☹	
	☺ 😐 ☹	
	☺ 😐 ☹	
	☺ 😐 ☹	
	☺ 😐 ☹	
	☺ 😐 ☹	
	☺ 😐 ☹	

People I met

Notes

Sip . Smile . Write . Repeat

Sip . Smile . Write . Repeat

Winery name

Winery location

Wine I tasted	*I liked it, or not*	*Price per bottle*
	😊 😐 ☹	$
	😊 😐 ☹	
	😊 😐 ☹	
	😊 😐 ☹	
	😊 😐 ☹	
	😊 😐 ☹	
	😊 😐 ☹	
	😊 😐 ☹	
	😊 😐 ☹	
	😊 😐 ☹	

People I met

Notes

Sip. Smile. Write. Repeat

Sip . Smile . Write . Repeat

Winery name

Winery location

Wine I tasted	I liked it, or not	Price per bottle
	☺ 😐 ☹	$
	☺ 😐 ☹	
	☺ 😐 ☹	
	☺ 😐 ☹	
	☺ 😐 ☹	
	☺ 😐 ☹	
	☺ 😐 ☹	
	☺ 😐 ☹	
	☺ 😐 ☹	
	☺ 😐 ☹	

People I met

Notes

Sip . Smile . Write . Repeat

Sip . Smile . Write . Repeat

Winery name

Winery location

Wine I tasted	I liked it, or not	Price per bottle
	🙂 😐 ☹	$
	🙂 😐 ☹	
	🙂 😐 ☹	
	🙂 😐 ☹	
	🙂 😐 ☹	
	🙂 😐 ☹	
	🙂 😐 ☹	
	🙂 😐 ☹	
	🙂 😐 ☹	
	🙂 😐 ☹	

People I met

Notes

Sip . Smile . Write . Repeat

Sip . Smile . Write . Repeat

Winery name

Winery location

Wine I tasted	I liked it, or not	Price per bottle
	☺ 😐 ☹	$
	☺ 😐 ☹	
	☺ 😐 ☹	
	☺ 😐 ☹	
	☺ 😐 ☹	
	☺ 😐 ☹	
	☺ 😐 ☹	
	☺ 😐 ☹	
	☺ 😐 ☹	
	☺ 😐 ☹	

People I met

Notes

Sip . Smile . Write . Repeat

Sip . Smile . Write . Repeat

Winery name

Winery location

Wine I tasted	I liked it, or not	Price per bottle
	☺ 😐 ☹	$
	☺ 😐 ☹	
	☺ 😐 ☹	
	☺ 😐 ☹	
	☺ 😐 ☹	
	☺ 😐 ☹	
	☺ 😐 ☹	
	☺ 😐 ☹	
	☺ 😐 ☹	
	☺ 😐 ☹	

People I met

Notes

Sip . Smile . Write . Repeat

Sip . Smile . Write . Repeat

Winery name

Winery location

Wine I tasted	I liked it, or not	Price per bottle
	☺ 😐 ☹	$
	☺ 😐 ☹	
	☺ 😐 ☹	
	☺ 😐 ☹	
	☺ 😐 ☹	
	☺ 😐 ☹	
	☺ 😐 ☹	
	☺ 😐 ☹	
	☺ 😐 ☹	
	☺ 😐 ☹	

People I met

Notes

Sip . Smile . Write . Repeat

Sip . Smile . Write . Repeat

Winery name

Winery location

Wine I tasted	I liked it, or not	Price per bottle
	☺ 😐 ☹	$
	☺ 😐 ☹	
	☺ 😐 ☹	
	☺ 😐 ☹	
	☺ 😐 ☹	
	☺ 😐 ☹	
	☺ 😐 ☹	
	☺ 😐 ☹	
	☺ 😐 ☹	
	☺ 😐 ☹	

People I met

Notes

Sip . Smile . Write . Repeat

Sip . Smile . Write . Repeat

Winery name

Winery location

Wine I tasted	I liked it, or not	Price per bottle
	☺ 😐 ☹	$
	☺ 😐 ☹	
	☺ 😐 ☹	
	☺ 😐 ☹	
	☺ 😐 ☹	
	☺ 😐 ☹	
	☺ 😐 ☹	
	☺ 😐 ☹	
	☺ 😐 ☹	
	☺ 😐 ☹	

People I met

Notes

Sip . Smile . Write . Repeat

Sip . Smile . Write . Repeat

Winery name

Winery location

Wine I tasted	I liked it, or not	Price per bottle
	☺ 😐 ☹	$
	☺ 😐 ☹	
	☺ 😐 ☹	
	☺ 😐 ☹	
	☺ 😐 ☹	
	☺ 😐 ☹	
	☺ 😐 ☹	
	☺ 😐 ☹	
	☺ 😐 ☹	
	☺ 😐 ☹	

People I met

Notes

Sip . Smile . Write . Repeat

Sip . Smile . Write . Repeat

Winery name

Winery location

Wine I tasted	I liked it, or not	Price per bottle
	☺ 😐 ☹	$
	☺ 😐 ☹	
	☺ 😐 ☹	
	☺ 😐 ☹	
	☺ 😐 ☹	
	☺ 😐 ☹	
	☺ 😐 ☹	
	☺ 😐 ☹	
	☺ 😐 ☹	
	☺ 😐 ☹	

People I met

Notes

Sip. Smile. Write. Repeat

Sip . Smile . Write . Repeat

Winery name

Winery location

Wine I tasted	I liked it, or not	Price per bottle
	☺ 😐 ☹	$
	☺ 😐 ☹	
	☺ 😐 ☹	
	☺ 😐 ☹	
	☺ 😐 ☹	
	☺ 😐 ☹	
	☺ 😐 ☹	
	☺ 😐 ☹	
	☺ 😐 ☹	
	☺ 😐 ☹	

People I met

Notes

Sip. Smile. Write. Repeat

Sip . Smile . Write . Repeat

Winery name

Winery location

Wine I tasted	*I liked it, or not*	*Price per bottle*
	☺ 😐 ☹	$
	☺ 😐 ☹	
	☺ 😐 ☹	
	☺ 😐 ☹	
	☺ 😐 ☹	
	☺ 😐 ☹	
	☺ 😐 ☹	
	☺ 😐 ☹	
	☺ 😐 ☹	
	☺ 😐 ☹	

People I met

Notes

Sip . Smile . Write . Repeat

Sip . Smile . Write . Repeat

Winery name
_____

Winery location
_____

Wine I tasted	I liked it, or not	Price per bottle
	☺ 😐 ☹	$
	☺ 😐 ☹	
	☺ 😐 ☹	
	☺ 😐 ☹	
	☺ 😐 ☹	
	☺ 😐 ☹	
	☺ 😐 ☹	
	☺ 😐 ☹	
	☺ 😐 ☹	
	☺ 😐 ☹	

People I met
_____

Notes
_____

Sip . Smile . Write . Repeat

Sip . Smile . Write . Repeat

Winery name
___

Winery location
___

Wine I tasted	I liked it, or not	Price per bottle
	☺ 😐 ☹	$
	☺ 😐 ☹	
	☺ 😐 ☹	
	☺ 😐 ☹	
	☺ 😐 ☹	
	☺ 😐 ☹	
	☺ 😐 ☹	
	☺ 😐 ☹	
	☺ 😐 ☹	
	☺ 😐 ☹	

People I met
___

Notes
___
___

Sip . Smile . Write . Repeat

Sip . Smile . Write . Repeat

Winery name

Winery location

Wine I tasted	I liked it, or not	Price per bottle
	☺ 😐 ☹	$
	☺ 😐 ☹	
	☺ 😐 ☹	
	☺ 😐 ☹	
	☺ 😐 ☹	
	☺ 😐 ☹	
	☺ 😐 ☹	
	☺ 😐 ☹	
	☺ 😐 ☹	
	☺ 😐 ☹	

People I met

Notes

Sip . Smile . Write . Repeat

Sip . Smile . Write . Repeat

Winery name

Winery location

Wine I tasted	I liked it, or not	Price per bottle
	☺ 😐 ☹	$
	☺ 😐 ☹	
	☺ 😐 ☹	
	☺ 😐 ☹	
	☺ 😐 ☹	
	☺ 😐 ☹	
	☺ 😐 ☹	
	☺ 😐 ☹	
	☺ 😐 ☹	
	☺ 😐 ☹	

People I met

Notes

Sip . Smile . Write . Repeat

Sip . Smile . Write . Repeat

Winery name

Winery location

Wine I tasted	I liked it, or not	Price per bottle
	☺ 😐 ☹	$
	☺ 😐 ☹	
	☺ 😐 ☹	
	☺ 😐 ☹	
	☺ 😐 ☹	
	☺ 😐 ☹	
	☺ 😐 ☹	
	☺ 😐 ☹	
	☺ 😐 ☹	
	☺ 😐 ☹	

People I met

Notes

Sip . Smile . Write . Repeat

Sip . Smile . Write . Repeat

Winery name
___

Winery location
___

Wine I tasted	I liked it, or not	Price per bottle
	😊 😐 ☹	$
	😊 😐 ☹	
	😊 😐 ☹	
	😊 😐 ☹	
	😊 😐 ☹	
	😊 😐 ☹	
	😊 😐 ☹	
	😊 😐 ☹	
	😊 😐 ☹	
	😊 😐 ☹	

People I met
___

Notes
___
___

Sip . Smile . Write . Repeat

Sip . Smile . Write . Repeat

Winery name

Winery location

Wine I tasted	I liked it, or not	Price per bottle
	😊 😐 ☹	$
	😊 😐 ☹	
	😊 😐 ☹	
	😊 😐 ☹	
	😊 😐 ☹	
	😊 😐 ☹	
	😊 😐 ☹	
	😊 😐 ☹	
	😊 😐 ☹	
	😊 😐 ☹	

People I met

Notes

Sip. Smile. Write. Repeat

Sip . Smile . Write . Repeat

Winery name

Winery location

Wine I tasted	*I liked it, or not*	*Price per bottle*
	☺ 😐 ☹	$
	☺ 😐 ☹	
	☺ 😐 ☹	
	☺ 😐 ☹	
	☺ 😐 ☹	
	☺ 😐 ☹	
	☺ 😐 ☹	
	☺ 😐 ☹	
	☺ 😐 ☹	
	☺ 😐 ☹	

People I met

Notes

Sip . Smile . Write . Repeat

Sip . Smile . Write . Repeat

Winery name

Winery location

Wine I tasted	*I liked it, or not*	*Price per bottle*
	☺ 😐 ☹	$
	☺ 😐 ☹	
	☺ 😐 ☹	
	☺ 😐 ☹	
	☺ 😐 ☹	
	☺ 😐 ☹	
	☺ 😐 ☹	
	☺ 😐 ☹	
	☺ 😐 ☹	
	☺ 😐 ☹	

People I met

Notes

Sip . Smile . Write . Repeat

Sip . Smile . Write . Repeat

Winery name

Winery location

Wine I tasted	I liked it, or not	Price per bottle
	😊 😐 ☹	$
	😊 😐 ☹	
	😊 😐 ☹	
	😊 😐 ☹	
	😊 😐 ☹	
	😊 😐 ☹	
	😊 😐 ☹	
	😊 😐 ☹	
	😊 😐 ☹	
	😊 😐 ☹	

People I met

Notes

Sip . Smile . Write . Repeat

Sip . Smile . Write . Repeat

Winery name
_____

Winery location
_____

Wine I tasted	I liked it, or not	Price per bottle
	☺ 😐 ☹	$
	☺ 😐 ☹	
	☺ 😐 ☹	
	☺ 😐 ☹	
	☺ 😐 ☹	
	☺ 😐 ☹	
	☺ 😐 ☹	
	☺ 😐 ☹	
	☺ 😐 ☹	
	☺ 😐 ☹	

People I met
_____

Notes
_____
_____

Sip . Smile . Write . Repeat

Sip . Smile . Write . Repeat

Winery name

Winery location

Wine I tasted	I liked it, or not	Price per bottle
	☺ 😐 ☹	$
	☺ 😐 ☹	
	☺ 😐 ☹	
	☺ 😐 ☹	
	☺ 😐 ☹	
	☺ 😐 ☹	
	☺ 😐 ☹	
	☺ 😐 ☹	
	☺ 😐 ☹	
	☺ 😐 ☹	

People I met

Notes

Sip . Smile . Write . Repeat

Sip . Smile . Write . Repeat

Winery name

Winery location

Wine I tasted	I liked it, or not	Price per bottle
	☺ 😐 ☹	$
	☺ 😐 ☹	
	☺ 😐 ☹	
	☺ 😐 ☹	
	☺ 😐 ☹	
	☺ 😐 ☹	
	☺ 😐 ☹	
	☺ 😐 ☹	
	☺ 😐 ☹	
	☺ 😐 ☹	

People I met

Notes

Sip . Smile . Write . Repeat

Sip . Smile . Write . Repeat

Winery name
___

Winery location
___

Wine I tasted	I liked it, or not	Price per bottle
	☺ 😐 ☹	$
	☺ 😐 ☹	
	☺ 😐 ☹	
	☺ 😐 ☹	
	☺ 😐 ☹	
	☺ 😐 ☹	
	☺ 😐 ☹	
	☺ 😐 ☹	
	☺ 😐 ☹	
	☺ 😐 ☹	

People I met
___

Notes
___
___

Sip . Smile . Write . Repeat

Sip . Smile . Write . Repeat

Winery name

Winery location

Wine I tasted	I liked it, or not	Price per bottle
	☺ 😐 ☹	$
	☺ 😐 ☹	
	☺ 😐 ☹	
	☺ 😐 ☹	
	☺ 😐 ☹	
	☺ 😐 ☹	
	☺ 😐 ☹	
	☺ 😐 ☹	
	☺ 😐 ☹	
	☺ 😐 ☹	

People I met

Notes

Sip . Smile . Write . Repeat

Sip . Smile . Write . Repeat

Winery name

Winery location

Wine I tasted	I liked it, or not	Price per bottle
	☺ 😐 ☹	$
	☺ 😐 ☹	
	☺ 😐 ☹	
	☺ 😐 ☹	
	☺ 😐 ☹	
	☺ 😐 ☹	
	☺ 😐 ☹	
	☺ 😐 ☹	
	☺ 😐 ☹	
	☺ 😐 ☹	

People I met

Notes

Sip . Smile . Write . Repeat

Sip . Smile . Write . Repeat

Winery name

Winery location

Wine I tasted	I liked it, or not	Price per bottle
	☺ 😐 ☹	$
	☺ 😐 ☹	
	☺ 😐 ☹	
	☺ 😐 ☹	
	☺ 😐 ☹	
	☺ 😐 ☹	
	☺ 😐 ☹	
	☺ 😐 ☹	
	☺ 😐 ☹	
	☺ 😐 ☹	

People I met

Notes

Sip . Smile . Write . Repeat

Sip . Smile . Write . Repeat

Winery name

Winery location

Wine I tasted	I liked it, or not	Price per bottle
	☺ 😐 ☹	$
	☺ 😐 ☹	
	☺ 😐 ☹	
	☺ 😐 ☹	
	☺ 😐 ☹	
	☺ 😐 ☹	
	☺ 😐 ☹	
	☺ 😐 ☹	
	☺ 😐 ☹	
	☺ 😐 ☹	

People I met

Notes

Sip. Smile. Write. Repeat

Sip . Smile . Write . Repeat

Winery name

Winery location

Wine I tasted	I liked it, or not	Price per bottle
	😊 😐 ☹	$
	😊 😐 ☹	
	😊 😐 ☹	
	😊 😐 ☹	
	😊 😐 ☹	
	😊 😐 ☹	
	😊 😐 ☹	
	😊 😐 ☹	
	😊 😐 ☹	
	😊 😐 ☹	

People I met

Notes

Sip . Smile . Write . Repeat

Sip . Smile . Write . Repeat

Winery name

Winery location

Wine I tasted	I liked it, or not	Price per bottle
	☺ 😐 ☹	$
	☺ 😐 ☹	
	☺ 😐 ☹	
	☺ 😐 ☹	
	☺ 😐 ☹	
	☺ 😐 ☹	
	☺ 😐 ☹	
	☺ 😐 ☹	
	☺ 😐 ☹	
	☺ 😐 ☹	

People I met

Notes

Sip . Smile . Write . Repeat

Sip . Smile . Write . Repeat

Winery name

Winery location

Wine I tasted	I liked it, or not	Price per bottle
	☺ 😐 ☹	$
	☺ 😐 ☹	
	☺ 😐 ☹	
	☺ 😐 ☹	
	☺ 😐 ☹	
	☺ 😐 ☹	
	☺ 😐 ☹	
	☺ 😐 ☹	
	☺ 😐 ☹	
	☺ 😐 ☹	

People I met

Notes

Sip . Smile . Write . Repeat

Sip . Smile . Write . Repeat

Winery name

Winery location

Wine I tasted	I liked it, or not	Price per bottle
	☺ 😐 ☹	$
	☺ 😐 ☹	
	☺ 😐 ☹	
	☺ 😐 ☹	
	☺ 😐 ☹	
	☺ 😐 ☹	
	☺ 😐 ☹	
	☺ 😐 ☹	
	☺ 😐 ☹	
	☺ 😐 ☹	

People I met

Notes

Sip. Smile. Write. Repeat

Sip . Smile . Write . Repeat

Winery name

___

Winery location

___

Wine I tasted	I liked it, or not	Price per bottle
	😊 😐 ☹	$
	😊 😐 ☹	
	😊 😐 ☹	
	😊 😐 ☹	
	😊 😐 ☹	
	😊 😐 ☹	
	😊 😐 ☹	
	😊 😐 ☹	
	😊 😐 ☹	
	😊 😐 ☹	

People I met

___

Notes

___

___

Sip . Smile . Write . Repeat

Sip . Smile . Write . Repeat

Winery name

Winery location

Wine I tasted	I liked it, or not	Price per bottle
	☺ 😐 ☹	$
	☺ 😐 ☹	
	☺ 😐 ☹	
	☺ 😐 ☹	
	☺ 😐 ☹	
	☺ 😐 ☹	
	☺ 😐 ☹	
	☺ 😐 ☹	
	☺ 😐 ☹	
	☺ 😐 ☹	

People I met

Notes

Sip . Smile . Write . Repeat

Sip . Smile . Write . Repeat

Winery name

Winery location

Wine I tasted	I liked it, or not	Price per bottle
	☺ 😐 ☹	$
	☺ 😐 ☹	
	☺ 😐 ☹	
	☺ 😐 ☹	
	☺ 😐 ☹	
	☺ 😐 ☹	
	☺ 😐 ☹	
	☺ 😐 ☹	
	☺ 😐 ☹	
	☺ 😐 ☹	

People I met

Notes

Sip . Smile . Write . Repeat

Sip . Smile . Write . Repeat

Winery name

Winery location

Wine I tasted	I liked it, or not	Price per bottle
	☺ 😐 ☹	$
	☺ 😐 ☹	
	☺ 😐 ☹	
	☺ 😐 ☹	
	☺ 😐 ☹	
	☺ 😐 ☹	
	☺ 😐 ☹	
	☺ 😐 ☹	
	☺ 😐 ☹	
	☺ 😐 ☹	

People I met

Notes

Sip . Smile . Write . Repeat

Sip . Smile . Write . Repeat

Winery name

Winery location

Wine I tasted	I liked it, or not	Price per bottle
	😊 😐 ☹	$
	😊 😐 ☹	
	😊 😐 ☹	
	😊 😐 ☹	
	😊 😐 ☹	
	😊 😐 ☹	
	😊 😐 ☹	
	😊 😐 ☹	
	😊 😐 ☹	
	😊 😐 ☹	

People I met

Notes

Sip . Smile . Write . Repeat

Sip . Smile . Write . Repeat

Winery name

Winery location

Wine I tasted	I liked it, or not	Price per bottle
	☺ 😐 ☹	$
	☺ 😐 ☹	
	☺ 😐 ☹	
	☺ 😐 ☹	
	☺ 😐 ☹	
	☺ 😐 ☹	
	☺ 😐 ☹	
	☺ 😐 ☹	
	☺ 😐 ☹	
	☺ 😐 ☹	

People I met

Notes

Sip . Smile . Write . Repeat

Made in the USA
Monee, IL
31 July 2024

63044507R00056